Musical Instruments

Ukulele

By Nick Rebman

level 1 little blue readers

www.littlebluehousebooks.com

Little Blue House is distributed by North Star Editions:
sales@northstareditions.com | 888-417-0195

Produced for Little Blue House by Red Line Editorial.

Photographs ©: Shutterstock Images, cover, 4, 7, 9, 11, 13, 17, 19, 21, 23, 24 (top left), 24 (top right), 24 (bottom left), 24 (bottom right); iStockphoto, 14–15

Library of Congress Control Number: 2022911115

ISBN
978-1-64619-703-3 (hardcover)
978-1-64619-735-4 (paperback)
978-1-64619-796-5 (ebook pdf)
978-1-64619-767-5 (hosted ebook)

Printed in the United States of America
Mankato, MN
012023

About the Author

Nick Rebman is a writer and editor who lives in Minnesota. He enjoys reading, walking his dog, and playing rock songs on his drum set.

Table of Contents

My Ukulele

I play my ukulele.

It makes a nice sound.

The ukulele has
four strings.
Each one makes a
different sound.

string

I play my ukulele outside.

I use one hand to strum.

I put my other hand on the neck.

I press the strings while I strum.

neck

I have a teacher.

He shows me how to play different notes.

teacher

I practice with
my teacher.
She teaches me a
new song.

I practice on a bench.

I get better every day.

I practice with my dad.

He claps while I play.

I practice with my mom.

I sing while I play.

I play with my friend.
We love making
music together.

Glossary

clap

strings

friend

teacher

Index